25 TRUTHS YOU NEVER HEARD IN CHURCH

D1383974

25 TRUTHS YOU NEVER HEARD IN CHURCH

Becoming a
Kingdom-Focused Believer

by

Dr. Joseph Mattera

Powered by eGenCo   Generation Culture Transformation
                     Specializing in publishing for generation culture change

eGenCo
824 Tallow Hill Road
Chambersburg, PA 17202, USA
Phone: 717-461-3436
Email: info@micro65.com
Website: www.micro65.com

facebook.com/egenbooks

youtube.com/egenpub

egen.co/blog

pinterest.com/eGenDMP

twitter.com/eGenDMP

instagram.com/egenco_dmp

Publisher's Cataloging-in-Publication Data
Mattera, Joseph
25 Truths You Never Heard in Church. Becoming a
Kingdom-focused Believer.; by Dr. Joseph Mattera.
72 pages cm.
ISBN: 978-1-68019-859-1 paperback
        978-1-68019-860-7 ebook
        978-1-68019-861-4 ebook
1. Christianity. 2. Salvation. 3. Kingdom of God.
I. Title
2017934835

Interior design by Versatile PreMedia Services, Pune, India

TABLE OF CONTENTS

Truth # 1   The Bible's main theme is not the church or Israel, but the Kingdom of God.   3

Truth # 2   The Cultural Mandate is the key to interpreting the Bible.   6

Truth # 3   The Metanarrative of Scripture is the Kingdom.   10

Truth # 4   All believers are called to full-time ministry.   13

Truth # 5   The world awaits the manifestation of the sons of God.   17

Truth # 6   The true purpose of being born again is to experience the Kingdom of God.   19

Truth # 7   John 3:16 is not just about individual salvation.   21

Truth # 8   Only Kingdom-focused prayers are answered.   23

Truth # 9   The Bible is not a book about heaven.   25

Truth # 10   When we receive Jesus as Lord, we also receive Jesus our Creator.   28

Truth # 11   The Bible teaches common grace as well as saving grace.   30

Truth # 12   The incarnation of Christ is a model for our whole life.   32

Truth # 13 The political language of the Kingdom implies cultural engagement. 34

Truth # 14 The church is "the ground and pillar of the truth." 37

Truth # 15 We are to labour for both revival and reformation. 39

Truth # 16 The Trinity provides a model for human authority under divine Headship. 40

Truth # 17 The Bible does not teach a "rights-centered" gospel. 42

Truth # 18 The Great Commission is corporate, not just for individual sinners. 43

Truth # 19 In the Kingdom the pastor is a shepherd of his community. 45

Truth # 20 The highest levels of spiritual strongholds are ideological. 46

Truth # 21 We need to model the city of God in our congregation before we can change the world. 48

Truth # 22 We need theological transformation before we can experience societal transformation. 49

Truth # 23 Only transformed leaders can transform the world. 50

Truth # 24 Only a desperate, hungry remnant will bring lasting transformation. 52

Truth # 25 A congregation is only as strong as their marriages because a church is a family of families. 54

Introduction

As we shift from an individualistic gospel to the gospel of the Kingdom, our eyes are opened and we not only view life differently but also have a radically new and vibrant understanding of the Bible. I found this out firsthand more than two decades ago when I transitioned from a classical (fundamentalist) Pentecostal paradigm to a (holistic) Kingdom view. Aside from radically altering my understanding of Scripture, it profoundly affected my preaching, transformed the worldview of our local church, and gave birth to a worldwide ministry. For the first seventeen years of my Christian experience, my understanding of the Bible was limited to an individual salvation message of faith in Christ, repentance and forgiveness of sins, divine healing, deliverance, and victory over the devil. These five components of our salvific experience are essential, but should only be a foundational starting point for believers.

The message of the Kingdom enlarges the scope of the individualistic gospel (not eradicating but expanding its implications) so that believers are compelled to positively affect communities, cities, and nations. As a matter of fact, the gospel of the Kingdom can navigate believers away from narcissism, since it shifts the focus off of the individual and onto the surrounding community. Believers go from merely *escaping* the world to *engaging* the world. The Kingdom message brings practical application to everyday life. At the same time, it brings conviction to believers so that they consider how to apply the gospel to loving their neighbours and serving humanity. This is because every kingdom has social systems (politics, education, business, law, family, music, arts, science, religion, entertainment, etc.) that enable it to legitimately function as a kingdom.

In the Gospels Jesus told us to pray for His Kingdom to come and His will to be done on earth as it is in heaven (Mt. 6:10; Lk. 11:2). Hence, Jesus' purpose and mission was

1

not only the salvation of individual sinners, but reconciling the created order back to Himself (see Col. 1:20). The implications in this are profound! For example, can you imagine what would happen if the 30-million-plus evangelical believers in the U.S.A. all had a Kingdom mind-set instead of an individual understanding of salvation? Can you imagine the difference it would make if every megachurch in the nation preached and practiced the gospel of the Kingdom? Sadly, many megachurches do not positively affect the quality of life in their own communities. While they may be megachurches in terms of crowds, they have minor influence in terms of their impact on the surrounding culture.

Ever since the church, beginning in the late 19th century, essentially replaced the gospel of the Kingdom with an individualistic gospel, believers increasingly have abandoned nurturing the gatekeepers of culture and have left the elite institutions of higher learning in the hands of the secular humanists. The result has been the continual erosion of biblical morality, which may eventuate in the elimination of freedom of religion in North America and beyond. Contrariwise, can you imagine how many more people we would be able to bring to Christ if we preached the gospel of the Kingdom? The reason why is because under a Kingdom mindset, every believer is a minister of God sent into the world to bring their particular sphere of influence into alignment under the Lord Jesus.

My primary goal in writing this book is to change the mindset of believers to embrace the gospel of the Kingdom. I believe we need a theological transformation before we will ever see a societal reformation. The prophet Hosea said God's people are destroyed because of a lack of knowledge (Hos. 4:6). Thus, in this book I am attacking biblical and Kingdom ignorance and sharing some critical truths that many of you who are reading this probably have never heard in a typical church service.

Truth # 1

The Bible's main theme is not the church or Israel, but the Kingdom of God.

Your kingdom come, your will be done, on earth as it is in heaven (Matthew 6:10).

First of all, we need to ask ourselves the question: "What is the Kingdom of God?" As I understand it from Scripture, the Kingdom of God is the rule or government of God that emanates from the personal throne of God in heaven. There are two major aspects of God's Kingdom (or government) in the universe. One is the general sovereign rule of God that controls and maintains order through common grace and natural law throughout the whole universe. Passages of Scripture that teach this include Colossians 1:17, "...in him all things hold together"; Psalm 24:1, "The earth is the LORD's and the fullness thereof"; Psalm 22:28, "For kingship belongs to the Lord, and he rules over the nations"; and Daniel 4:34-35, "...his dominion is an everlasting dominion...he does according to his will among the host of heaven and among the inhabitants of the earth; and none can stay His hand..."

The second aspect of the Kingdom is the personal manifest Kingdom in which individuals and systems are aligned under His Lordship. This is what Jesus was referring to when He told us to pray for His Kingdom to come and His will to be done on earth as it is in heaven (Mt. 6:10). The reason why He used heaven as the primary reference for His Kingdom on earth was because in heaven the rebellion was squelched and Satan and his angels were thrown out (see Rev. 12: 7-9). Thus, in heaven there is no rebellion against God; its inhabitants and systems are completely aligned under His rule.

On earth, the starting point for this personal Kingdom alignment is salvation. People begin coming into alignment under Jesus and His Kingdom when they are born again of the Holy Spirit (see Jn. 3:3- 8). The moment a person experiences salvation, their sins are forgiven, their (spiritual) eyes are opened immediately, and they begin to see (experience, understand, and know) that Jesus is truly Lord over all and that His invisible Kingdom rules the visible universe! This shows how important it is that we present the gospel and convert people to Christ. Conversion is the starting point for enlisting saints in the Kingdom army. Consequently, the gospel of the Kingdom should not hinder world evangelism; it should only enhance it by giving believers an opportunity to be established in their faith with the purpose of being lights to the world.

In summary, anytime an individual, family, community, city, or nation comes under the rule of God (whether personally or in principle), we see a personal application of the Kingdom reality Jesus told us to pray for (see Lk. 11:2-4). To further clarify, the church is not the Kingdom, but the key agent of the Kingdom that represents God to this fallen world. Believers are to serve as the salt and light of the world (see Mt. 5:13 -16) that influences all other jurisdictions in the Kingdom. Thus, the church is called to displace the enemy and bring each jurisdiction or government to function under the Lordship of Christ. Many Roman Catholics, Orthodox, and evangelicals erroneously believe and/or behave as if the church is the Kingdom. This is impossible because the earth doesn't belong to the church, as Psalm 24:1 and other passages teach.

If you think I am making too big a deal about one aspect of Scripture–think again. The major theme of both the Old and New Testaments is the Kingdom of God. Regarding the New Testament, John the Baptist, Jesus, and Paul all preached the Kingdom, not the church. John said, "Repent, for the kingdom of heaven is at hand" (Mt. 3:2). Jesus went about "…preaching the gospel of the kingdom…" (Mt. 4:23 NKJV). The apostle Paul went about "…proclaiming the kingdom" (Acts 20:25). And Luke summarized Paul's ministry and preaching in Acts 26:30-31 by saying that he "…welcomed all who came to him, proclaiming the kingdom of God and teaching about the Lord Jesus Christ…"

These passages, and more, demonstrate that the church is called not only to win souls, but also to transform systems, communities, and nations. Since the word "kingdom" means "the king's domain," and Jesus wanted His domain on the earth as it is in heaven, it points back to the "Cultural Mandate" found in Genesis 1:28.

This is rarely ever preached to a congregation during Sunday services.

Truth # 2

The Cultural Mandate
is the key to interpreting the Bible.

God said to them, "Be fruitful and multiply; fill the earth and subdue it; have dominion over the fish of the sea, over the birds of the air, and over every living thing that moves on the earth" (Genesis 1:28 NKJV).

I have said for many years that Genesis 1:26-28 is the most important passage in the Bible, especially when it comes to understanding our purpose in Christ. Without these verses we cannot understand the reason for our birth or the purpose of Israel, the church, or the coming of Christ. Why? Because we cannot understand the purpose of God unless we frame the whole of Scripture with Genesis 1:28 as our interpretive lens. Scholars apply various designations to these verses, such as the "covenant of creation," the "cultural mandate," the "cultural commission," and the "dominion mandate." All of these descriptions are adequate, in my opinion, but for the sake of this book I will refer to it as the "Cultural Mandate."

The Cultural Mandate means that God called believers to bring His dominion (influence) into all of culture, not just the church. This is very important because it proves that the church is not the Kingdom. Rather, this command tells us to go into culture (all of creation) as our mission. If the church were the Kingdom, it would be akin to God telling Adam and Eve just to concentrate on nurturing plants in the safety of the Edenic garden. God told Adam, in essence, "Don't hang out in a safe place and don't create a holy ghetto, but reach every sphere of society and bring all realms under My rule." This is an important principle to understand because in it we discover that believers are not only called to focus on Sunday ministry.

For those of you who object, consider this: the Cultural Mandate is the first command given to Adam by God mentioned in Scripture. This is why some refer to it as the "Covenant of Creation." Since Adam and Eve were our Federal heads, this command represented the will of God for all those in covenant with Him. Secondly, to any who say that this command is no longer in effect because of the fall of man, God repeats the Cultural Mandate to Noah almost verbatim (see Gen. 9:1-2). Although the words are slightly different, the essence is the same.

There are others who insist that this command to cultivate and rule the earth was given generically to all men, saved or unsaved. My response is that Noah was in covenant with God and there is no passage of Scripture elsewhere in which the Cultural Mandate is given to an unbeliever. Of course, Satan desires to rule the world and will attempt to have dominion through fallen men, but this is an act of rebellion against God, not the result of God granting fallen humankind the right to rule autonomously without aligning under the Lord Jesus. Hence, we cannot understand the divine rebooting of the "post flood" world through Noah unless we first start with the original covenant God made with Adam and Eve in Genesis 1:28.

Furthermore, I propose that the Cultural Mandate connects all subsequent covenants, including the New Covenant. For example, without the Genesis 1:26 - 28 framework, it is impossible to understand the Abrahamic Covenant, when God promised Abram that "…in you all the families of the earth shall be blessed" (Gen. 12:3). Why? Because when the Cultural Mandate was given to Adam and Noah, there were no nations; the earth was not fully populated at that time. By the time Abram came on the scene, however, there were multitudes of people on the earth that formed many nations. Thus, the Cultural Mandate, as applied to nations, was that God's blessing (blessing comes through His dominion or alignment under His Kingdom) would come through covenant families.

God also told Abraham that out of his own loins would arise kings and princes who would possess the gates of their enemies (see Gen. 17:5-7; 22:17-18). Sounds a lot like the Cultural Mandate in that the seed of Abraham is called to be the gatekeepers of culture. This also has implications for the New Covenant, since Galatians 3:29 teaches that those in Christ are Abraham's seed. Hence, the church is called to influence the halls of cultural power. (The "gates" are a metaphor for the seat of power in a city, similar to the White House in the U.S.A. or City Hall where a city mayor conducts business; see Prov. 31:23.)

After the nation of Israel was established, God gave Moses a promise that sounded much like the Cultural Mandate. In Deuteronomy 28:13, God told Israel He was going to make them "...the head and not the tail; you shall be above only, and not be beneath..." (NKJV) God spoke through David and prophesied that the coming Messiah would inherit all the nations as His inheritance (see Ps. 2:8). As the last Adam (1 Cor. 15:45), Jesus came to fulfil the original commandment that God gave the first Adam in Genesis 1:28 to have dominion over the created order. This of course points the mission of Jesus back to the Cultural Mandate.

One of the last recorded sayings of Christ before He ascended into heaven is known as the Great Commission. In Matthew 28:19 Jesus commissions believers to disciple the nations, which many scholars say is the New Testament equivalent to the Cultural Mandate of Genesis 1:28. The word nation in this passage does not refer to an individual "ethnic" but a particular people group or nation. These passages demonstrate that both Testaments were framed with a call to influence the whole world, not just the church.

The Great Commission is a mandate to use the Bible as a blueprint to build civil society, not just win individual souls. The chronological beginning, middle, and end of the Bible have a topical thread that cannot be interpreted without the Cultural Mandate. For example, even Isaiah the prophet said of the Messiah, "...of the increase of His government and peace There shall be no end" (Isaiah 9:7 NKJV). The whole Bible points to God's Kingdom as the metanarrative (or major story) of Adam, the patriarchs, the law, the prophets, and the New Testament.

In all my years as a Christian I have never heard anyone teach or preach this.

Truth # 3

The Metanarrative
of Scripture is the Kingdom.

...making known to us the mystery of his will, according to his purpose, which he set forth in Christ as a plan for the fullness of time, to unite all things in him, things in heaven and things on earth. In him we have obtained an inheritance, having been predestined according to the purpose of him who works all things according to the counsel of his will (Ephesians 1:9-11).

Those of you who enjoy movies know that every movie has two basic components that make it interesting: a major theme and various subplots. For example, if you are watching a movie about WWII, it usually doesn't get right to the point regarding who won and lost the battle; it is replete with subplots that make it interesting. Subplots may include romance, conflict between two of the major characters, the relationship between characters and their loved ones, the inner conflict that arises when one character has to kill another human being, etc. Sometimes these subplots are so good that it is easy to lose track of the main theme of the movie!

Recently I have come to the conclusion that most of the body of Christ today are building their ministries on subplots. By subplots I mean things like deliverance, healing, prosperity, and family. Although all these subjects are very important, they are only subplots in God's overall redemptive story. So what is the metanarrative (main plot) of God's redemptive story? Ephesians 1:9-11 summarizes it: that all things, both in heaven and in earth, be united together in Christ. This is where all of human history is heading. This is the culmination of the cross and the resurrection, and is the purpose of the church.

The critical clue in this passage is the phrase, "a plan for the fullness of time." God's main objective from the beginning was to unite "all things" in Christ by sending His Son to redeem man and reconcile creation back to Him. In other words, the Lordship of Christ over all is the macro theme or narrative of Scripture and human history, and is the purpose of Christ's redemption of humankind. Since Christ is the "last Adam," (1 Cor. 15:45), this passage points right back to the Cultural Mandate of Genesis 1:28.

Any vision or ministry that doesn't point towards the Lordship of Christ over all creation will find itself fighting against God, because Ephesians 1:11 says that God "works all things according to the counsel of His will." Any person or ministry that is focused on a subplot and/or their own vision takes away from God's ultimate objective and therefore will not maximize their divine purpose. What are the implications of this? They are vast! It means that most Christian ministries, including church planting movements, Bible schools, discipleship programs, family ministries, and evangelistic endeavours, are focusing on a subplot, which is why we are not seeing the Cultural Mandate fulfilled.

Another implication is that the Kingdom of God compels the church to espouse a biblical worldview in every cultural mountain in order to walk in God's purpose of uniting all things together in Christ. Hence, we cannot merely disciple businesspeople without teaching them the biblical purpose of wealth creation (see Deut.8:18). We cannot merely disciple scientists with the individual salvation message without pointing them to the fact that science is God's "67th book" (both the New and Old Testament books equal 66) so they can use science to discover and declare the glory of God (see Ps. 19; Rom. 1:19-23).

You get the picture. Pastors and leaders in every local church and ministry need to understand the general framework of what the Bible says in every cultural mountain so that they can equip the saints in every sphere of life with the purpose of aligning their particular vocation systemically under biblical principles. In order to do this, believers are called to think God's thoughts after Him as His image bearers on the earth (see Gen. 1:26-27). Consequently, it behooves every believer to take the study of Scripture seriously, especially those called to teach the Word.

We can no longer afford merely to establish people in the faith with subplot teachings. We need to have a biblical framework in a general sense so we can equip the future gatekeepers of society. This takes much discipline and study. (For help on this, read my books *Ruling in the Gates*, *Kingdom Revolution*, and *Kingdom Awakening*, which give a biblical worldview in every major arena of life.) To conclude, when preachers separate the gospel from the Kingdom they then make the gospel only about individual blessing which, although important, is still only a subplot to the the main theme of God's Word and plan.

I have never heard this preached by a pastor while I have been in church.

Truth # 4

All believers
are called to full-time ministry.

And He Himself gave some to be apostles, some prophets, some evangelists, and some pastors and teachers, for the equipping of the saints for the work of ministry… (Ephesians 4:11-12a NKJV)

Once we truly understand the gospel of the Kingdom, both our biblical concepts and descriptions are changed for the good. For example, I no longer say that a person is in "full-time" ministry when referring to church ministry. I say, full-time "church" ministry so as to not make an unnecessary and misleading distinction between church and marketplace when it comes to the ministry. According to the New Testament, all believers are called to be equipped for the work of the ministry (see Eph. 4:12). Not all are called to function in full-time church ministry, but everyone is called to represent God as His minister, irrespective if they preach in a church or not. To minister means simply to serve, regardless of vocation.

The context of "the work of ministry" is found in Ephesians 4:10, which says that the purpose of the ascension of Christ was to "fill all things." Thus, the context shows that the work of the ministry is to equip the saints likewise to fill all things; that is to say, to lead in every sphere of society. After the first message of the church on the Day of Pentecost, 3,000 were saved; but they had no church buildings to attend. It was a decentralized move of God in which believers went to the temple to learn from the apostles, but then used their homes to break bread and build each other up (see Acts 2:46). The present institutionalized method of church in which all the activity takes place within a large edifice once per week is one reason why the church is not multiplying disciples in developed nations. The early church was primarily a believer's movement in which each convert organically spread the gospel in his or her community.

To unpack this further, we have to understand that the first move of the Holy Spirit on the earth was not on the Day of Pentecost when believers were baptized with the Holy Spirit and spoke in tongues (as most Pentecostals believe). The first move of the Spirit took place in the beginning, after God created the earth and the Spirit was hovering over creation (see Gen. 1:2). Thus, the Holy Spirit was attracted to God's work of creation. The truth is, the Holy Spirit is still attracted to creativity in His image-bearers (see Gen. 1:27). This means that whenever believers utilize their natural abilities and creativity (as God designed) in their vocation (plumbing, architecture, law, music, art, politics, social work, military strategy, sports, etc.) then they attract God's Spirit. Hence, all believers can expect to be filled with the power of the Holy Spirit every time they function from Monday through Saturday, not just on Sunday.

For instance, if you are called to be a math professor, then every time you teach mathematical equations you can be filled with the Holy Spirit because obedience to your God-given vocation is an act of worship. As a matter of fact, *avodah* is the transliteration of the Hebrew word for both *worship* and *work*. In the Hebraic biblical mind-set faith and work integrate. That being said, believers do not have to wait until they are in Sunday church services to worship and be filled with the Spirit. Once we as believers understand these realities they will liberate us forever! We will no longer go to work with drudgery, but be filled with joy as we understand we are fulfilling our God-given assignment just as much as our pastor is when he is preaching on Sunday.

As I conclude this chapter, let's review a snapshot of history to see how some of this bifurcation between church and marketplace ministry took place. In 787 A.D., a great schism began to develop (which became a complete break in 1054 A.D.) between the Eastern and Western church. The West insisted on the addition of the phrase to the Nicene Creed about how the Holy Spirit proceeded from both the Father and the Son, while the East said He proceeded only from the Father. *Filioque* is a Latin word meaning "and the Son," which was added to the Nicene-Constantinopolitan Creed by the Church of Rome in 1054 A.D., one of the major factors leading to the Great Schism between East and West.

Consequently, this seemingly minor addition of "and the Son" had huge implications, since many in the West started believing that the Holy Spirit was not working in a people group or culture until the gospel was preached. However, we see from Genesis 1:2 that the Spirit has been at work even before a church was established or the gospel was preached to an unchurched nation or people. The Spirit has been working in each of us even before we were saved or heard the gospel as well. Hence, God is already imbedded in every culture and ethnic group, even those who have not heard the gospel.

Thus, those of us who preach the gospel of the Kingdom have great faith that He is already at work in every culture, nation, and system of the world. We just have to discern which biblical keys will unlock the door to their hearts. Furthermore, when you understand the Kingdom of God you realize that God has been at work in your life since before you were naturally born (see Jer. 1:5; Eph. 1:4), not just after you were born again and received Christ. God honors all the work He did in your life, even before you came to faith in Christ. This is because He is the one who endowed you with all your natural gifts fit to serve Him in your particular vocation.

When we separate the gospel from the Kingdom we honour only our post-conversion life because we only understand how the spiritual gifts and anointing work in church-related ministry. However, the Kingdom is about reaching every sphere with the gospel, which means that we celebrate our natural gifts and abilities given from birth, not only our spiritual gifts.

I have never heard my pastor teach this in any of our church gatherings.

Truth # 5

The world awaits
the manifestation of the sons of God.

For the creation waits with eager longing for the revealing of the sons of God (Romans 8:19).

According to Romans 8:19-23, all of creation is awaiting the manifestation of the (mature) sons of God. They are not looking for the best political system or universities, but for the church to mature. The Greek word for sons in this passage is *huios*, which means a mature son in the household. This is different from another Greek word (teknon) used in Romans 8:16-17, which refers to children that have not yet come of age to be considered mature sons. The most that can be said about children in this passage is that they know they are saved! Why? Because this is the starting point towards mature sonship; it is not the end all.

As long as believers view Christianity as a rights-centered gospel they will remain children, which is why we have not yet transformed nations. We need our congregations to transition from children to mature sons, which has to do with those who are responsible stewards for their Father. Creation is not waiting for mere children or babes (see 1 Cor. 3:1-3 for a description of a babe in Christ); they await the manifestation of the mature sons of God! In order to nurture mature sons (in the New Testament, sons include both male and female converts), we need to stop preaching a narcissistic gospel and embrace the gospel of the Kingdom that serves communities, instead of producing crowds of people who want God to serve them. Furthermore, it is only the sons of God that are truly led by the Spirit of God (see Rom. 8:14). This has huge implications, since it refers to the fact that God cannot trust mere children with His plans and directives. It also implies the absolute essential focus of the church on making disciples instead of having crowds of Christians. The Greek term for "disciple" in the New Testament is *mathetes*, which refers to a person who adheres completely to the teachings of Christ, weaving it into his rule of life and conduct.

Truth is, Jesus called His serious followers disciples, not Christians (see Lk. 14:25-33). The secular world gave Christ-followers the name "Christian" (see Acts 11:26), and this term was only used twice in the New Testament (see Acts 11:26; 1 Pe. 4:16). In contrast, the word "disciple" is used more than 100 times to describe Christ-followers. The top priority of most ministries today is to gather crowds and persuade unbelievers to make so-called "decisions for Christ." This in spite of the fact that Jesus never command-ed the church to make new converts; He commanded us to make disciples (see Mt. 28:19). Of course, this obviously includes evangelism and winning them to Christ in order to begin the maturation process.

Disciple-making is the lost art of the church today. It doesn't matter how large your church or how big your bud-get—what matters most is how many true disciples you are making for the Lord. Furthermore, disciple-making is the only proven way to nurture believers into becoming mature sons of God. Finally, in order for you to effectively make disciples, you have to be a disciple of another leader. There are no exceptions. If you are not aligned under a leader, then you will have a hard time getting others to be properly aligned under you!

This is something that is rarely, if ever, taught to congre-gations in church gatherings.

Truth # 6

The true purpose of being born again is to experience the Kingdom of God.

Truly, truly, I say to you, unless one is born again he cannot see the kingdom of God (John 3:3).

For the first seventeen years of my Christian life, I espoused a gospel limited to individual redemption and salvation. Hence, I did not correctly interpret Scriptures regarding the Kingdom of God because I was blinded by my theology. As a result, for all those years I put limitations on passages that were beyond the scope of my paradigm. I was not alone. Before the year 2000, very few people in the body of Christ understood, much less preached, the gospel of the Kingdom. Consequently, thousands of evangelists preached that you must be born again in order to go to heaven. But this is not what the text is saying, is it? Read it again.

Being born again has nothing to do with heaven. In this verse Jesus is saying that when we are born again, our spiritual eyes are opened and we have the insight to discern that this world is under the Lordship of Christ. Remember, the word "kingdom" means "the king's domain," and the whole world belongs to the Lord! (see Ps. 24:1). What this implies is that being born again is the starting point for enlisting us in the army of God to bring every sphere back to the Father. We realize for the first time that the whole universe really belongs to God and that those not in submission to Him are spiritual rebels. It also refers to the fact that when we are born again, we begin to get attuned to the fact that the invisible spiritual Kingdom is more powerful and ultimately rules over the visible kingdoms of this world.

So to summarize, being born again has nothing to do with a believer experiencing a geographical transition to another place (heaven). The Kingdom (God's rule) is just as much a reality in the natural world of the universe as it is in the spiritual heavenly realms. Being born again starts in the here and now, on this side of heaven, not on the other side. Being born again has to do with understanding and experiencing the Kingdom of God. Of course, Christ-followers will eventually have access to everything in the heavenly realms; however, being born again is more about heaven coming inside of us than of us going to heaven. It is not about going to heaven but about bringing heaven down to earth, as Jesus told us to pray (see Mt. 6:9).

In all my years as a believer, I do not remember anyone preaching this in a church service.

Truth # 7

John 3:16
is not just about individual salvation.

For God so loved the world, that he gave his only Son, that whoever believes in him should not perish but have eternal life (John 3:16).

In 1978 I had my "first" conversion to Jesus as my personal Lord and Savior, but in 1995 I experienced my "second" conversion—to the gospel of the Kingdom! As a result, I have spent the years since then reading the Bible with Kingdom glasses on. To this day, I am still unpacking the biblical implications of this second conversion, which is the thesis of this book. I began re-reading all the popular passages we all take for granted, and I was astonished at the new, expansive meaning I had!

For example, one of the most popular passages in the Bible is John 3:16. Before my conversion to the Kingdom, I understood this passage as merely referring to an individual person receiving Christ, being forgiven, and going to heaven. Again, this is not what it says when you read it with "Kingdom glasses" on. Heaven is not mentioned–neither is forgiveness of sins–although both are incorporated as part of salvation.

Presently, I understand John 3:16 as not just God loving individual sinners, but sending His Son to redeem the created order ("world" in the Greek is *kosmos*, which is the systems of the created order). Thus *kosmos* is the ordered universe, the natural laws of God's creation, as well as the habitat and order of things in human civilization. Hence, God not only loves the people of the world, but also the systems that support the people in the world.

Secondly, this passage says, "whoever believes in him should not perish." I used to say that this merely meant that a person who believes in Jesus would not go to hell. Of course, that is the ultimate destination of all unbelievers. However, the word "perish" in the Greek is *appollsyai*, which means to be ruined, marred, be lost, which in essence means to miss its purpose. This is the same word used in Mark 2:22 when Jesus said that if new wine is put inside old wineskins it will perish. Of course, wineskins do not go to hell, and in this context the wineskin still exists in the earth realm but cannot be used any more to hold wine.

"Believe" in this passage doesn't merely mean making a decision for Christ or intellectual ascent; "believe" is an action word and also means obedience to God.

Thus, when we put on Kingdom glasses we now interpret John 3:16 like this: God so loved the kosmos (the people and the systems that support the people on the earth) that He gave His Only Son (who is the King of His Kingdom), that whoever obeys Him will be directly aligned under Him in His Kingdom and will fulfil their purpose in this world. This expanded meaning astonished me and revolutionized how I preached this popular passage! Hence, this passage not only deals with individual salvation but incorporates God's Kingdom purpose for His people in the created order.

This is something I have never heard taught in a church or ministry gathering.

Truth # 8

Only Kingdom-focused prayers are answered.

Your Kingdom come, your will be done, on earth as it is in heaven" (Matthew 6:9).

After my second conversion into Kingdom understanding, I re-read the Lord's Prayer and was shocked at how much more I got out of it! I learned that if our prayers are not Kingdom-focused, we are then not praying according to the will of God. I learned that much of the body of Christ is praying incorrectly because the first thing they mention when they approach God is their own personal needs. By contrast, as we read "the Lord's Prayer" (Mt. 6:9-13), we find that the framework Jesus laid out showed that worship and praying about the needs of His Kingdom should be our first focus before we even deal with our daily bread. (Daily bread represents our personal needs.)

Matthew 6:6-9 (NKJV) reads as follows:

Our Father in heaven, Hallowed be Your name. Your kingdom come. Your will be done On earth as it is in heaven. Give us this day our daily bread, And forgive us our debts, As we forgive our debtors. And do not lead us into temptation, But deliver us from evil. For Yours is the kingdom and the power and the glory forever. Amen.

Since Jesus taught us to "seek first the kingdom of God and His righteousness, and all these things shall be added to you" (Mt. 6:33 NKJV), we need to understand that He was sharing that the Father expects us to be Kingdom-focused first, before all other things. What He is saying in this passage is that those who are Kingdom-focused will automatically have all their personal needs met. This is why in the Lord's Prayer Jesus told believers to start praying for God's will and God's Kingdom. God can only trust those who have His Kingdom agenda as their primary focus in life. Consequently, those who only serve God to be personally blessed, and those who pray only to receive something from God, are missing the point and probably will rarely receive God's fullness in this life.

Of course, this is a far cry from the focus of most of the preaching today in the body of Christ. Most of the teachings we hear on prayer and faith have to do with understanding how to obtain individual blessings based on our rights in Christ. This is all fine and good, as far as it goes. However, according to how Jesus taught us to pray, using prayer first and foremost to have our needs met is not in line with Kingdom priorities. It also doesn't comport with Jesus' teaching in Matthew 6:33 when He told us not to put personal needs ahead of seeking first His Kingdom. If we as believers are going to maximize our calling and transform the world, we have to put God's desires and will ahead of our own when it comes to prayer.

I have never heard anyone preach this in church.

Truth # 9

The Bible is not a book about heaven.

Your kingdom come, your will be done, on earth... (Matthew 6:10)

Although most Christians think that the Bible is primarily about spiritual things and heaven, the fact is that it is primarily a book about stewarding the earth. For example, the law, the prophets, the psalms, and the rest of the wisdom literature, are all about living out our faith on the earth. In the Gospels, Jesus taught His followers to be the salt of the earth and the light of the world (see Mt. 5:13-14), not the salt of the church and the light of heaven. He also said that the meek would inherit the earth (see Mt. 5:5). In addition, the Book of Acts, the epistles of Paul, Peter, and Jude, and the Book of Hebrews are all about how to live for God on the earth. Even the Book of Revelation has to do with the sovereign rule of God directing the affairs of men on the earth.

The Bible doesn't even say that much about heaven. This is because our primary assignment from the birth of humanity had to do with the Cultural Mandate of bringing God's influence upon all of creation (see Gen. 1:28). Unfortunately, after the church shifted from preaching the gospel of the Kingdom to preaching about the end times and the rapture in the 1880s, it went from focusing on the earth to escaping the earth and looking for heaven. This has severely skewed our biblical interpretation.

For example, we have redefined ministry to mean full-time church ministry, which includes the planting of churches, preaching, handling the sacraments of communion and water baptism, and performing sacerdotal duties such as conducting weddings and funerals. (Things that are very important indeed!) However, all believers are in ministry and function as priests of the Lord, according to 1 Peter 2:8-9. Every believer in the workplace is a Christian minister, not just full-time church ministers. (Not everyone is a sacerdotal minister, but all believers are Christian ministers.) Hence, we need to put on Kingdom glasses when we read the Bible so we can interpret the Bible accurately.

For example, the fivefold ministry gifts found in Ephesians 4:11—apostle, prophet, evangelist, pastor, and teacher—are called to equip God's people for the work of the ministry (see Eph. 4:12). However, once we understand the Kingdom, we can discover the holistic meaning of this passage by looking at the context, which includes Ephesians 4:10, which says that Jesus ascended to "fill all things." Thus, this contextual understanding shows that the fivefold ministry gifts were empowered by Christ as gifts to the church to equip God's people to fill all things.

So we can conclude that all believers are called to be ministers, representing God in this world to fulfil the Cultural Mandate (see Gen. 1:28) of repopulating the earth ("filling all things") so that the Lordship of Christ is over all. Thus, the church should nurture and produce ministers of God in government, law, economics, education, music, art, entertainment, media, the military, sports, etc., and not just church ministers. Moreover, even marketplace leaders may have a fivefold function if they are equipped by fivefold church ministers (see Eph. 4:11) who reproduce their anointing in their disciples; however, they still need to submit to their spiritual leaders in the ecclesial realm when it comes to the things related to the church.

In conclusion, the church should equip believers for all of life, not just church life. Their mission should be the community, not just church gatherings on Sunday. The primary focus of Sunday gatherings should be to win people to Christ and equip the saints for the work of the ministry, which is to fill all things. The greatest proof that the church is alive and vibrant is when its members positively affect their surrounding communities through the presence and love of God.

In all my years as a believer, I have never heard anyone preach the contents of this chapter.

Truth # 10

When we receive Jesus as Lord, we also receive Jesus our Creator.

All things were made through Him, and without Him nothing was made that was made (John 1:3 NKJV).

The Jesus we received in our heart for salvation is both our Redeemer (see Jn. 1:12-13) and Creator of the cosmos (see Jn. 1:3). This truth is profound because it obligates the church to both love and serve Jesus, as well as His Creation. In all my years in the church, and after listening to thousands of teachings, I have never heard anybody make this connection before! This truth shows that both the natural and spiritual worlds equally belong to God. Consequently, the spiritual versus physical dualism so often preached in the church is not biblical because it separates Jesus as Redeemer from Jesus as Creator.

The fact that Jesus became human flesh demonstrates that the natural is not inherently evil. Human flesh only became the embodiment of sin after the fall of Adam (see Gal. 5:16-17); however, in addition to humanity, creation as a whole is the object of Christ's redemption (see Col. 1:20). For this reason, the church has an obligation to steward the created order as the priests/kings of the Creator. Hence, the church is called not only to equip believers for church ministry but also for marketplace ministry. Once we understand this, we also understand that the whole of creation—not just the church—is the sanctuary of God (see Ps. 24; 104).

Once we embrace the Kingdom message, we will not only send people out to be pastors, but also to be scientists, sociologists, anthropologists, geologists, botanists, administrators of communities and cities, and every other legitimate career or profession we can imagine, because the created order was originally planted by Jesus.

In all my years in the church I have never heard this preached!

Truth # 11

The Bible teaches common grace as well as saving grace.

...be sons of your Father who is in heaven. For he makes his sun rise on the evil and on the good, and sends rain on the just and on the unjust (Matthew 5:45).

Many years ago, my ministry approach was transformed when I realized that there was a difference between "saving grace" and "common grace." Saving grace is only for the elect, those born-again believers who are baptized by Christ into the body of Christ. Common grace is the blessings that emanate from the throne of God on both the righteous and the wicked, such as the shining sun and the rain Jesus mentions in Matthew 5:45. The world would fall apart without common grace because Jesus gives light (truth and knowledge) to every man coming into the world (see Jn. 1:4, 9). This means that the ability to provide political leadership in the administration of cities, states, and nations; create new technologies; understand science and natural law; devise and execute military and police strategies; function in economics; perform with excellence in language, music, art, and education; and develop and demonstrate athletic prowess at the highest level, all come from God's common grace.

His common grace supports the humans He created so that there is a civilization made up of systems that support and sustain the people living on the earth. John 1:4, 9 are profound passages that state that Jesus gives light to all men, not just saved men. Romans 13:1, 4 teach us that even the pagan Roman political authorities in Paul's time were put in place by God as His servants. The Greek word for servant in Romans 13:4, (*diakonos*), is the same word used elsewhere in the New Testament to mean "deacon." Political leaders, for example, are endowed with God's common grace to be His deacons to administrate cities and bring peace and order to communities so the gospel can be preached (see 1 Ti. 2:1-4).

Isaiah chapter 45 prophesied about 300 years ahead of time that a Persian king named Cyrus would allow the Jews to return to Jerusalem from exile in order to rebuild that city. Consequently, this chapter refers to this unsaved pagan king as God's anointed and chosen one. At the end of the day, all men ultimately do God's bidding because He works all things according to the counsel of His will (see Eph. 1:11). The reason why this is so important is because it releases believers to partner with their local, state, and national elected officials—their mayors, governors, senators, president—for the good of their community, even though those officials may not be Christians.

Before I understood this truth, I had a difficult time working with those who did not know the Lord because I thought it was a waste of time, almost like being unequally yoked with an unbeliever. Once God illuminated me, I was free to work with all leaders, irrespective of their political affiliation, ideology, or lifestyle. This does not mean I endorse their lifestyle or beliefs; it merely means I recognize them as God's deacons, endowed by Him to serve their community.

This is something I have never heard preached in all my years in church!

Truth # 12

The incarnation of Christ
is a model for our whole life.

For most of my years in the church I only heard about the need for all men to receive Jesus as their Savior (see Jn. 1:12). But, except for the yearly Christmas message related to the birth of Christ, I do not recall ever hearing a message regarding the Word becoming flesh and dwelling among us, as found in John 1:14. However, this passage speaks not merely of His birth, but of His entire life on the earth, which lasted more than thirty-three years!

As Christ-followers, we are not only to bask in the heavenly blessings we receive in Christ as a result of His death, burial, and resurrection (see 1 Cor. 1:30-31; Eph. 1:3), but we are also called to imitate His whole life (see Mt. 5-7). Consequently, the Word becoming flesh provides a missional lesson for the church regarding our need to be immersed in the mission field to which we are called. God did not merely send the Word (ideas or concepts), but embodied the Truth in human flesh. He became flesh to save and serve the ones He was assigned to (see Heb. 2:14-18).

This deeper understanding of the incarnation obligates us not only to celebrate the birth of Christ during Christmas, but also to present our bodies as a living sacrifice for our divine vocation (see Rom. 12:1-2). Those of us called to at-risk communities are not merely called to "march for Jesus," but to "move in" for Jesus and immerse ourselves into the neighbourhoods of our flock. It is not usually enough for our church building to be in the community; the incarnation compels us to live among the people we are called to.

I tell people all the time that the safest place to be is not some nice affluent suburb, but in the will of God. No matter where you are called to serve, the will of God is always the safest place for your spouse and children (see Ps. 91).

In closing, we in the church need to hear more about the life and times of Jesus, and not just about His birth and the last six hours of His life as He hung on the cross. Why? Because God has provided us with the most effective model for evangelization: the incarnation.

This is something I never heard preached from a pastor during a Sunday church service.

The political language
of the Kingdom
implies cultural engagement.

...on this rock I will build my church, and the gates of hell shall not prevail against it (Matthew 16:18).

People often ask me whether or not the church should be involved in politics. My usual response is to ask, "Don't you know that the very first mention of the church in the New Testament uses a political word?" When Jesus says to Peter in Matthew 16:18 that He will build His church upon the rock, the Greek word used for "church" is *ecclesia*. This was a political word used to describe Greek citizens who assembled to vote and enact public policy (used first in Sparta around 687 B.C.). Even in the later New Testament we see the word used twice in Acts 19 to denote secular citizens coming together as the *ecclesia* to deal with economic issues in the city of Ephesus (see Acts 19:32, 41). Hence, Jesus borrowed a well-known political word to depict His followers. Consequently, the word "church" doesn't merely mean "the called out ones," as most seminaries and pastors preach, but to come together to lead or govern.

Furthermore, Jesus affirmed to Pilate that He came to earth to be King (see Jn. 18:37). John the revelator goes even further and says that His divine title is "King of kings and Lord of lords" (Rev. 19:16), a title also spoken of by Paul the apostle (see 1 Ti. 6:15). Thus, if you put His title together with what He called His followers (the *ecclesia*), Jesus essentially was calling for a new political order with Himself as the King (of His Kingdom) above all other kings, including the Roman emperor, and His followers serving as His congress or parliament, similar to the Roman Senate of His times. The term "king of kings" was also a familiar term in those days since the Kings of the East called themselves king of kings and god of gods. The Roman Caesar was also called the king of kings. Even the Persian king who fought against the Spartan warriors in the movie *300* called himself the king of kings.

In light of the above, we can see that the real reason why Jesus was crucified was because He was considered a threat to the rule of the Roman Caesar. Hence, Jesus was crucified for political reasons, not religious reasons (see Jn. 19:12-16). The first-century church was also persecuted because they preached that Jesus was Lord over Caesar (see Acts 17:7). This was also the reason why King Herod put all the babies two years old and under to death when he heard that the King of the Jews (Jesus) had been born (see Mt. 2:1-16).

To make it even more political, Jesus commissioned His *ecclesia* (church) to assail the gates of hell. As we saw earlier, gates represent where the elders and kings made decisions for public policy in a city, like City Hall or the White House in the U.S.A. (see Pro. 31:23 and Gen. 22:17.) Consequently, Jesus was saying that His Kingdom would have followers under His reign who would eventually overturn ungodly and unjust social systems that formed the infrastructure of the nations they would disciple (which would happen when the church would baptize whole nations, as we read in Matthew 28:19-20).

The gospel (good news) was proclaimed by messengers throughout the Empire whenever the firstborn son of the Roman Caesar was born. Hence, when Jesus sent out His disciples to proclaim the good news of the Kingdom of God, He was also showing that a new King with His Kingdom was now on the scene. This was perceived as a huge political threat to the Roman system of government. He also called His twelve main disciples apostles (see Mk. 3:14), which was the title of Roman generals who were sent out leading a cadre of battleships to conquer new territories for Rome and set up an *ecclesia* (a ruling body representing Rome to the people) in the conquered cities.

Finally, the mountains that Jesus said could be removed by faith (see Mk. 11:23) were most likely the seven mountains built by King Herod in Jerusalem to signify his power. Removing them in this passage could have referred to removing the unjust Roman power over the church through faith in God.

As we put all of the above in context we have to conclude that if Jesus came today and preached the same concepts, He would still be murdered by unjust, power-hungry elites!

I have never heard this preached in a church gathering!

Truth # 14

The church is
"the ground and pillar of the truth."

*...the house of God, which is the church of the living God, the
pillar and ground of the truth* (1 Timothy 3:15 NKJV).

In 1 Timothy 3:15, St. Paul calls the church "...the ground
and pillar of the truth."

When you approach the gospel strictly from an individualistic salvation paradigm, this passage refers only to the
church being the guardian of biblical truth. However, once
you are baptized into an understanding of the Kingdom, the
biblical meaning of this verse is vastly expanded to include
all of culture and creation, not just the church. The implications of this are huge.

I believe this passage says that the church is called, as the
salt of the earth and light of the world, to be the prophetic
arbiters of truth regarding ethics, science, family, politics,
and economics in a civil society, not only arbiters of the
truth related to church biblical doctrine. When the church
has enough power to frame societal ethics, then there will be
a limit to the sleazy movies put out by Hollywood; pro-abor-
tion laws will be eradicated; a plumb line will be established
regarding the definition of marriage and family; and a limit
will be set as to how far science can go regarding the cloning
of living things and robotics.

Unfortunately, because the typical pastor only focuses
on issues regarding his congregation, secular progressive
humanists have long since framed societal ethics. However,
once the church embraces the gospel of the Kingdom, this
passage will cause them to again delve into every aspect of
culture so they can be the prophetic voice into all aspects
of culture. This passage also implies the need for numerous

Kingdom think tanks, and for believers to be nurtured to serve as public intellectuals and theologians, with the wisdom to interpret and apply the word of God to contemporary culture. Finally, 1 Timothy 3:15 further unpacks the fact that the church is the hope of the world as representatives of the Kingdom who function as the salt and light of the world.

In all my years in the body of Christ I have never heard any spiritual leader share the truths in this chapter!

Truth # 15

We are to labour
for both revival and reformation.

For the earth will be filled with the knowledge of the glory of the LORD as the waters cover the sea (Habakkuk 2:14).

Once we come into the Kingdom message, we no longer focus solely on praying for revival and awakening. We understand that revival is not enough to shift culture because it only awakens the church and evangelizes sinners. Merely bringing people into the church without affecting the gatekeepers of each of the spheres of society will only result in larger churches with no cultural impact. Only when we reach and disciple the cultural elites in politics, economics, business, music, art, media, education, and science, can we shift the culture from ungodly to godly.

Without a Kingdom mindset we will merely get individuals saved and give them a vision for church-related ministry. This is why it is possible to have a megachurch with minor influence politically and socially in the surrounding community. However, when we have a Kingdom mindset we not only bring people into the church and save their souls, but we also send them out to serve their community as a minister of God. In the Kingdom, we not only nurture and send out pastors to plant churches, but also entrepreneurs to plant businesses, political and economic leaders to bring systemic change, and so forth.

Without the Kingdom message we have no way of teaching people to use their creativity in the marketplace to glorify and worship God. Truly, revival brings people into the church, but reformation sends people out of the church to transform society!

This is another biblical truth that is rarely taught in the church!

Truth # 16

The Trinity provides a model
for human authority
under divine Headship.

Go therefore and make disciples of all nations, baptizing them in the name of the Father and of the Son and of the Holy Spirit (Matthew 28:19).

Both the Old and New Covenants serve as blueprints for local faith communities to branch out and frame societies with a biblical worldview as salt and light. Although we believe in the separation of church and state because they are two separate spheres of authority in the created order, we do not believe in the separation of God and state, because all of life is about religious and moral choices. There is no such thing as moral neutrality; either society will be under the rule of a humanistic religious order or under a biblical religious order.

Understanding and applying the Triune Godhead to politics is extremely important. For example, the Godhead is the exemplar of the "one and the many" principle. This shows that there is one God in purpose and essence (ontology) but various expressions and functions related to each of the three personas of the Trinity. This lays the groundwork regarding the ability to strive for a unified community with functional accountability in the earth realm. Furthermore, because Jesus is God the Son, He models complete obedience to the Father that expresses oneness in the Triune Godhead. This submission of the ultimate God/human shows that, as Lord, even He as the King of kings submits to authority while at the same time all earthly rulers are ultimately in submission to His authority.

There will never be greater example of human perfection than what is found in the Son. Hence, all earthly rulers are to receive their ultimate governmental authority as derivative authority from the Son as long as they rule justly and reflect the general principles of His moral law. Thus, their right to lead is conditional. The moment they cease to represent the Son (as King of kings), their authority is illegitimate and the people have a right to hold them accountable and/or to remove them from leadership.

However, if Jesus was not God the Son but a god striving in an evolutionary ladder to become more and more like Father God (as the Mormons teach), then it can lead to tyrannically autocratic leadership (Because then it can imply that there can be other humans who are gods, striving to be equal to God -which earthly rulers can attribute to themselves and justify tyranny because they can claim divine rule over other humans). Mormons also claim to be gods like Jesus because they, like Jesus, are striving to be like God up the evolutionary ladder. Viewing Jesus as less than God strips Him of His ultimate human authority as King of kings.

Hence, only with a proper understanding of the biblical concept of the Triune Godhead do we have a framework for human government that limits the authority of human kings, leaders, and presidents.

This truth I have never heard in a sermon from a pastor or preacher in church.

Truth # 17

The Bible does not teach a "rights-centered" gospel.

God...gives you power to get wealth, that he may confirm his covenant that he swore to your fathers (Deuteronomy 8:18).

The "Word of Faith" and other Christian movements recently emphasized the believer's rights in Christ Jesus. While this is true, those who understand the Kingdom expand the meaning of "in Christ" to include stewardship. For example, while it is true that God wants to prosper believers materially (see 2 Jn. 3), Scripture also teaches that the primary reason for wealth is so His people can confirm His covenant in the earth (see Deut. 8:18). Furthermore, while Scripture teaches us that we have been blessed with all spiritual blessings in heavenly places (see Eph. 1:3), it also teaches that believers are seated with Christ in heavenly places. Seated has to do with sharing in His authority as King over the earth. Believers have a kingly function on the earth, not just a priestly function (see Rom. 5:17; Rev. 1:6), which means we are responsible for what goes on in the earth realm as His global body. Believers tend to focus more on their call as priests than their call as kings, possibly because they do not want the responsibility as His stewards, called to manage the planet.

When we fail to frame individual passages of Scripture with Genesis 1:28 as our primary assumption (which makes it clear believers are called to steward the created order), we tend to limit the Bible and apply it only for individual blessings.

Consequently, those who understand the Kingdom of God understand the "in Christ" passages to also imply stewardship rather than merely individual blessings and benefits.

In all my years, I have never heard a pastor say this in a sermon.

Truth # 18

The Great Commission is corporate, not just for individual sinners.

Go into all the world and preach the gospel to every creature (Mark 16:15 NKJV).

One of the greatest things that has ever happened to me was when I discovered that the implications of the Kingdom expanded the reach of every passage of Scripture.

Even my understanding of the so-called "Great Commission" passages was greatly affected! For example, I used to think Matthew 28:19 (to disciple nations) merely had to do with making disciples of individual ethnic people; however, further study showed that the word "nation" in the original Greek language had to do with discipling whole people groups, not just individuals. This shows that the Great Commission is not just about individual redemption, but corporate redemption and transformation for nations. Furthermore, even the Mark 16:15-18 passage related to salvation, healing, deliverance, and speaking in new tongues, can have a corporate interpretation. Or they could be two bookends of the gospel: one to save and disciple individuals (Mark 16), and the other (Matthew 28) to show that we must equip and send disciples to transform nations.

Mark 16 also points to the first part of the Genesis 1:28 Cultural Mandate (bear fruit, multiply and replenish the earth), which has to do with enlarging the family of God biologically and spiritually. And Matthew 28 points to the latter part of the Cultural Mandate, which has to do with subduing the earth and having dominion (believers training their children to fill every realm of culture as gatekeepers and workers resulting in the earth being aligned under God again). I first heard this correlation between the Great

Commission and the Cultural Mandate from Dutch Sheets when he taught at a conference.

In all my years as a Christian, I have never heard a pastor preach this from the pulpit on a Sunday (although I have heard it alluded to in leadership conferences).

Truth # 19

In the Kingdom the pastor is a shepherd of his community.

...the Lord appointed seventy also, and sent them two by two... into every city and place where He Himself was about to go (Luke 10:1 NKJV).

When pastors understands the Kingdom of God, they realize their call as both a king and a priest. This often results in them being aware that God is calling them to have influence beyond the four walls of their church building. Since my conversion to the Kingdom message, I have had much interaction with the top political leaders in my community and beyond, and have served as a member of our local community board. This is because I knew I was called to be a shepherd/elder to my city, not just our church. As a result, our church and ministries have had many great opportunities to serve our community and help improve the quality of life for thousands of people.

The early church focused on more than just their individual congregations; they turned the world system upside down (see Acts 17:6). These Kingdom-focused believers affected the spiritual, social, and economic environment of their cities (see Acts 19:21-41). When Paul preached, he also attempted to influence the top gatekeepers of a city. We see a perfect example of this in his sermon to the Areopagus (see Acts 17:19-34). Consequently, pastors should view themselves as shepherds to their community or city, not just their congregations.

This I never remember hearing in a congregational meeting from my pastor.

Truth # 20

The highest levels of
spiritual strongholds are ideological.

*For the weapons of our warfare are not carnal but mighty in God
for pulling down strongholds* (2 Corinthians 10:3 NKJV).

When I first came into the Kingdom message, I quickly realized that I was dealing with higher levels of spiritual authority, both angelic and demonic. Principalities and powers are the invisible forces behind the visible realm. These are not merely individual demons that we cast out of people, but rulers of nations and empires that influence kings, politics, and policies over a nation. When you preach only an individualistic gospel, you probably are dealing only with lower-level demons that deceive people. But when you preach and practice the Kingdom of God, you challenge the ruling deities over a region and therefore will experience greater levels of spiritual warfare.

These principalities erect strongholds made up of ideologies and patterns of thought that pervade the culture of a city (see 2 Cor. 10:3-5). Ephesians 6:10-13 teaches us that the church of that city was wrestling against principalities and powers. Acts 19 shows how this same church affected the social, economic, and political landscape of Ephesus, a city that was backed up by a demonic goddess-idol. Daniel chapters 9 and 10 show us that as Daniel was fasting and praying he was able to see the invisible princes (or principalities) that were fighting for dominance over nations and empires. Luke chapter 10 relates how Jesus saw Satan fall like lightning from heaven after the seventy went about proclaiming the Kingdom of God in different cities (see Lk. 10:1-19).

Paul says in Ephesians 3:8-10 that the wisdom of God is made known to the principalities and powers through the church. The word "principality" in this verse is the Greek word *arche*, from which we derive the word "archetype." An archetype is derived from classical Greek Platonic philosophy, which taught that there were invisible archetypes (or powers) behind the invisible world. Hence, Paul is teaching here that both archangels and demonic principalities take their lead from the church. They see what God is doing and saying by observing the true church. Consequently, if the church is not concerned with anything but Sunday gatherings, ruling demonic entities will control cities, regions, and nations. However, when the church preaches and practices the gospel of the Kingdom, it activates the archangels and enables them to remove the grip of power Satan has over systems and communities.

If we really want to effect change in a culture, we need to proclaim and practice the Kingdom of God in a region. Only the Kingdom of God deals with systemic realities and challenges the dark forces of evil that influence the political and economic realms. The individual gospel can involve casting demons out of people; the gospel of the Kingdom can involve casting demonic rulers out of systems!

In conclusion, this also illustrates how imperative it is for those who preach and practice the gospel of the Kingdom to immerse themselves with much individual and corporate fasting and prayer! When you preach the Kingdom of God, you will likely attract the attention of high-level principalities over cities and nations and the level of spiritual warfare will dramatically intensify.

I do not remember ever hearing this truth taught from the pulpit from a pastor in all my years as a believer.

Truth # 21

We need to model the city of God in our congregation before we can change the world.

But the Jerusalem above is free, which is the mother of us all (Galatians 4:26 NKJV).

The body of Christ is not only the family of God; we function also as a nation (see 1 Pe. 2:8-9). As a nation we are supposed to function with biblical government in both the church and biological families, which involves submission to spiritual authority (see Heb. 13:17; Eph. 5:22-6:4); rules of engagement when in conflict (see Mt. 18:15-17); and building according to the heavenly pattern (see Heb. 8:5; 1 Ti. 3:1-15). As such, we are called to model the city of God with Jesus as our head.

When the church misses the mark in this area and is out of order we are then not prepared to exercise authority in the outside world (see 1 Cor. 6:1-7). If we cannot model how a nation is supposed to function within the household or nation of God, how can we hope to disciple the nations of the earth? For example, if the household of God is filled with a lack of order, division, ego-centric leadership, church politics, and unhealthy relational dynamics, the disciples they send out as gatekeepers will replicate the same dysfunction in their leadership. A messenger is not greater than the one who sent him (see Jn. 13:16.)

The household of God is supposed to be the place where future leaders are formed and sent out to the world as agents of change. When the church is either impotent or out of whack, the surrounding culture will reflect this. As the church goes, so goes societal culture, as church history has shown over the past 2000 years.

This is another principle that probably is not often preached from the pulpit to congregations.

Truth # 22

We need theological transformation before we can experience societal transformation.

For as [a man] thinks in his heart, so is he (Proverbs 23:7 NKJV).

The Bible teaches us that "faith comes by hearing, and hearing by the word of God" (Rom. 10:17 NKJV). Believers will only believe God commensurate to what they hear preached by their spiritual leaders. If the preponderance of spiritual leaders in the world focus only on the rapture and personal piety to the neglect of the full message of the Kingdom of God, then millions of believers in the world will not be activated to their marketplace calling. Hence, we need to have a theological transformation before we can ever expect a societal transformation. That is to say, what is preached from the pulpit will directly impact what believers practice in society.

If the church only teaches believers to wait for the rapture, then believers will only use God to escape earthly realities rather than to challenge and transform them. If believers are only taught from the pulpit how the gospel affects their individual life, then they will not understand how to apply the gospel to the public square. If the church only makes disciples to serve in the church and neglects the call to equip the saints to serve in the community, then the church will be irrelevant and fail to function as the salt of the earth and the light of the world.

This statement bears repeating: We need to have a theological transformation before we can see societal transformation.

I do not recall this being preached in any congregational church service I have ever attended.

Truth # 23

Only transformed leaders can transform the world.

But grow in the grace and knowledge of our Lord and Savior Jesus Christ (2 Peter 3:18).

Often it is much easier to focus on changing the outside world (through politics and economics) than it is to allow God to transform us. I believe this is the reason why Jesus first taught us how to have godly character traits before He called us to function as the salt and light of the world (see Mt. 5:1-16). Jesus only trusted broken people who are meek to inherit the earth, peacemakers to be statesmen, and leaders who can mourn, since His representatives need to empathize with the suffering of others before He grants them a public platform. Truly, God surrounds power with problems and challenges so only broken people can attain true leadership and have lasting influence in the Kingdom. Consequently, if we are going to bring true and lasting change to other people, we ourselves need to be changed. We have to know God before we can make Him known. We have to be transformed before we can transform others.

The message of the Kingdom of God has complete balance. It deals not only with the reign of God in culture, but with the reign of God within the church. This should compel every Christ-follower to seek regular encounters with the risen Christ that will be so profound they will be the catalyst for others to experience the power and presence of His Kingdom (see Heb. 6:5). Truly, God's Spirit desires to positively affect the realms of the spirit, soul, and body (see 1 Th. 5: 23). Jesus said in Luke 17:21 that the Kingdom of God is within us. That is to say, the power of the Kingdom works first in the hearts of people before it affects the surrounding culture. It works from the inside out—without the use of physical manipulation and force—not from the outside in. (Unlike Marxism, which seeks to bring a societal utopia from the outside in by bringing its version of economic equity through the use of force and violent overthrow.) Only to the extent that we allow God to transform our life will we be able to transform others.

This is another lesson that I have rarely heard preached today in the church.

Truth # 24

Only a desperate, hungry remnant will bring lasting transformation.

Blessed are those who hunger and thirst for righteousness, For they shall be filled (Matthew 5:6 NKJV).

As a new believer in 1978, I naively thought that all Christians were hungry and thirsty for God. I thought that everyone I met in the church was a committed Christ-follower. One of the biggest shocks I had as a new Christian was about six months into my newfound walk when I discovered that I already knew the Scriptures better than most of the others in our circle. As a pastor since the early '80s, I have also discovered that the only people in the church who receive anything from God are the ones who are hungry and thirsty for Him. This is why Jesus said that they are blessed and will be filled (see Mt. 5:6).

I came to realize that no matter how anointed my preaching was, only a remnant of those present would ever really become true disciples of Christ. Jesus only promised to fill those who are hungry, not merely those who attend church services. Those who are not hungry for God are already satisfied by something or someone other than Christ—and He will send them away empty (see Lk. 1:53).

This is why God rarely (if ever) uses a moral majority, but instead raises up a holy minority to advance His Kingdom (see Gideon's army of 300 in Judges 7; Abraham's 318 trained servants that defeated several nations in Genesis 14:14; and the remnant of 7,000 that did not bow their knee to Baal during the time of Elijah the prophet in 1 Kings 19:18). Only the most committed in the Kingdom will experience the most satisfaction in Jesus. Also, only the most committed in the Kingdom will be used of God to advance His Kingdom.

This is something I have rarely heard taught in the church.

Truth # 25

A congregation is only as strong as their marriages because a church is a family of families.

If a man does not know how to rule his own house, how will he take care of the church of God? (1 Timothy 3:5 NKJV)

In my final chapter, I want to share one of the greatest lessons I have ever learned in the Kingdom. That lesson is that the church is primarily a household of households or a family of families. Hebrews 1:2 says that God spoke to the fathers by the prophets. Why? Because the fathers were the heads of households and tribes, and were the real leaders of the nation of Israel. They even had more power than the kings because they had the authority to crown and/or remove kings (see 2 Sam. 2:3-4; 5:3; 19:11; 20:1-2). This is why the apostle Paul told Timothy that if a man cannot manage his own family, he cannot manage the household of God (see 1Ti. 3:4-5).

Consequently, any congregation, regardless of size, is only as healthy as its marriages and families. What good is it if we win the world and lose our children? Also, how can a man be trusted to love Christ's bride (which is the church) if he cannot lay down his life for his wife (see Eph. 5:25)? Before there was human government, the nation of Israel, the law of Moses, and the church, there was the institution of marriage (see Gen. 2). Therefore, marriage is the foundation of human civilization, which is why Satan tries his hardest to attack marriage and family. This explains why he is attempting to redefine marriage and family in our culture through political and social processes. Unless we have a biblical standard for marriage and families there is no reference point for the body of Christ to manage the church and make disciples.

Because discipleship often involves re-parenting (especially in our contemporary society with many fragmented families), pastors and other spiritual leaders need to first function as spiritual parents before they can be effective preachers and teachers. If we don't teach people how to replicate healthy families in the church, how in the world will they be effective in the world? The present day charismatic movement in the body of Christ that focuses on attracting crowds with visceral worship experiences and great preaching will not cut it if they do not have healthy habit patterns conducive to nurturing their biological and spiritual families.

This is not to say that a leader has to have a perfect marriage and family. Nobody I know has a perfect marriage and perfect children. As a matter of fact, I believe ground zero in spiritual warfare has to do with marriage and family. I have noticed that the greatest and most intense warfare I have ever experienced has been for my marriage and family and for the families of other leaders. It is no coincidence that Satan did not show up to tempt Adam when he was alone walking in the Garden with the presence and person of God. Even though Adam was an intellectual genius (he was able to name all the animals in the world and create the first taxonomy for the animal kingdom, which made him the first zoologist) as well as a spiritual giant without sin, he was no threat to Satan until he got married.

Notice that Adam and Eve were made one flesh in Genesis 2:22-25, and Satan immediately showed up in the very next verse at the beginning of chapter 3! Why? Because as powerful as Adam was, he was no threat to Satan as long as he was unable to reproduce after his own kind. Only those who reproduce both biological and spiritual families that walk with God are a threat to Satan's kingdom. This is another lesson I have never heard preached from the pulpit in any church service.

In conclusion, I pray that these 25 points will go viral (whether through my book or otherwise) and that the present generation of emerging and current leaders will walk these principles out. I truly believe that only then will we be able to see the fulfilment of the purpose of God in Christ, which is the uniting together of all things in heaven and earth (both the invisible and visible world), as it says in Ephesians 1:9-11.

**Additional teachings and resources by
Dr. Joseph Mattera, can be found at**

www.josephmattera.org

Audio

https://soundcloud.com/josephmattera

**Other books by Joseph Mattera – Available
for purchase on Amazon**

Kingdom Revolution

Kingdom Awakening

Ruling In The Gates

Walk In Generational Blessings

Understanding The Wineskin of the Kingdom

An Anthology of Essays on Apostolic Leadership

Essays on Cutting Edge Leadership

Travail to Prevail

Connect with
Dr. Joseph Mattera at any of the following locations:

740 40TH STREET
BROOKLYN NY 11232, USA
718.436.0242 EXT. 13
INFO@JOSEPHMATTERA.ORG

Facebook: /josephmattera
Twitter: /josephmattera
YouTube: /josephmattera
Instagram: /joseph_mattera